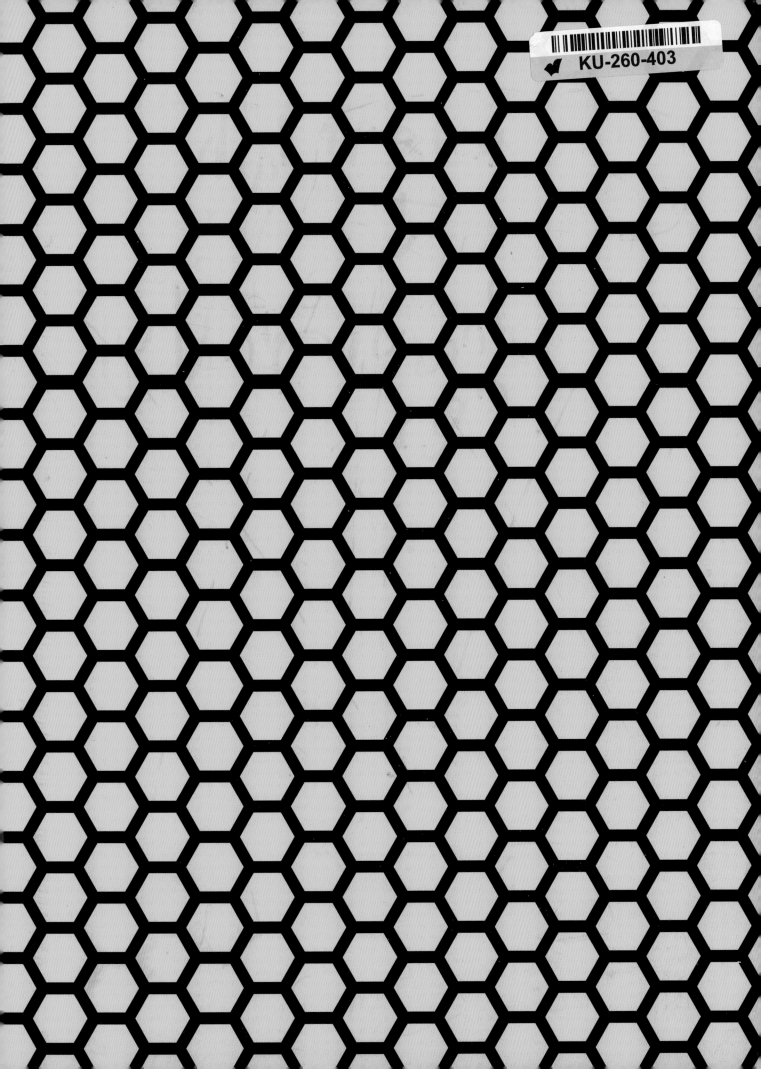

THIS JURASSIC WORLD DOMINION ANNUAL BELONGS TO:

....

I AM .... **YEARS OLD**

MY FAVOURITE DINOSAUR IS:

....

ORCHARD BOOKS

First published in Great Britain in 2022 by Hodder & Stoughton

A CIP catalogue record for this book is available from the British Library

ISBN 978 1 40836 848 0

1 3 5 7 9 10 8 6 4 2

FSC MIX Paper from responsible sources FSC® C104740

Printed and bound in China

Orchard Books
An imprint of Hachette Children's Group
part of Hodder & Stoughton Limited
Carmelite House
50 Victoria Embankment
London EC4Y 0DZ
An Hachette UK Company
www.hachette.co.uk
www.hachettechildrens.co.uk

ANNUAL 2023

ORCHARD

CONTENTS

BEWARE!

Dinosaurs roam the world! Herds of *Parasaurolophuses* graze peacefully on pasture land. Dangerous raptors hunt in the forests. Feathered pterosaurs the size of jet planes fly overhead. And watch out for the fearsome *T. rex* and the even bigger *Giganotosaurus*, the largest known land carnivore of all. You share the planet with them now. Take care out there!

A *T. rex* has been spotted nearby. Design a sign to warn others!

MEET... BLUE

Blue has always been the leader of her *Velociraptor* pack, hunting small mammals and dinosaurs. She has a long claw on the second toe of each foot that she uses to slash at prey before pinning them to the ground and biting them with her sharp teeth and powerful jaw. Now she has left the jungles of Isla Nublar, she must adapt and survive in a new environment. She lives in the pine woods in the Sierra Nevada mountains.

DINOSAUR INDEX

BLUE

BREED: *VELOCIRAPTOR* (VEL-OSS-IH-RAP-TOR)
MEANING: SWIFT THIEF
FAMILY: DROMAEOSAURIDAE

INTELLIGENCE: EXTREMELY HIGH

AGGRESSION: EXTREMELY HIGH

SUB-FILE: BETA
CLONE

CLASSIFIED

LENGTH
3.9m (12.79 ft)

1.7m (5.57 ft)

HEIGHT
1.88m (6.16 ft)

WEIGHT
226kg (500 lbs)

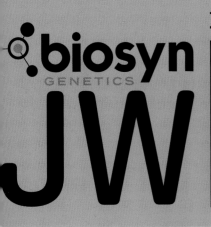

biosyn
GENETICS

JW

SE 04

RESEARCH
DIVISION

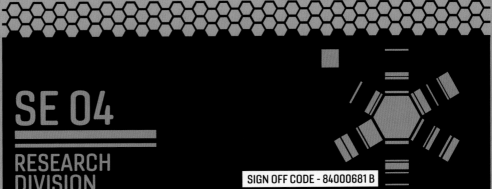

SIGN OFF CODE - 84000681 B

FOOTPRINT

DT5-9

EXT. 700

WORD SEARCH

Find and circle the *Jurassic World Dominion* character names in the word search below. The words can be horizontal, vertical, backwards or diagonal.

OWEN ☑ MAISIE ☐ CLAIRE ☐ ELLIE ☐ ALAN ☐ KAYLA ☐ IAN ☑

ANSWERS ON PAGE 60

D	B	I	O	N	M	A	Q	Z	D	X	H
E	K	C	I	Z	W	L	R	X	A	T	A
S	K	A	M	U	A	A	S	L	M	Z	S
C	G	K	Y	S	R	N	B	X	A	C	T
V	B	G	L	L	O	R	Q	T	I	O	S
O	W	E	N	S	A	M	G	S	S	T	O
X	Z	V	R	C	P	E	M	M	I	K	R
H	J	A	D	U	R	A	K	R	E	T	Z
Y	Z	E	Q	I	S	S	B	U	A	E	U
T	S	D	A	E	E	I	A	N	P	L	C
J	R	L	T	Z	B	G	H	J	K	A	Q
Z	C	S	C	V	B	E	L	L	I	E	S

BLUE AND BETA

MEET... BETA

A 1.2 m (4 ft) juvenile raptor, Beta is the mirror image and identical clone of her mother, Blue. Quick and alert, but still a bit clumsy on her legs, Beta learns how to hunt in the snowy hills of the Sierra Nevada mountain range, where she also encounters a new ally in thirteen year old Maisie. The two discover that the seemingly quiet surroundings are more threatening than they appear.

DINOSAUR INDEX

BETA

BREED: *VELOCIRAPTOR* (VEL-OSS-IH-RAP-TOR)
MEANING: SWIFT THIEF
FAMILY: DROMAEOSAURIDAE

INTELLIGENCE: HIGH

AGGRESSION: HIGH

LENGTH
1.2м (4 ft)

HEIGHT
1м (2.7ft)

HEIGHT
1.88M (6.16 ft)

WEIGHT
50 lbs

DT5-9

EXT. 700 CLASSIFIED

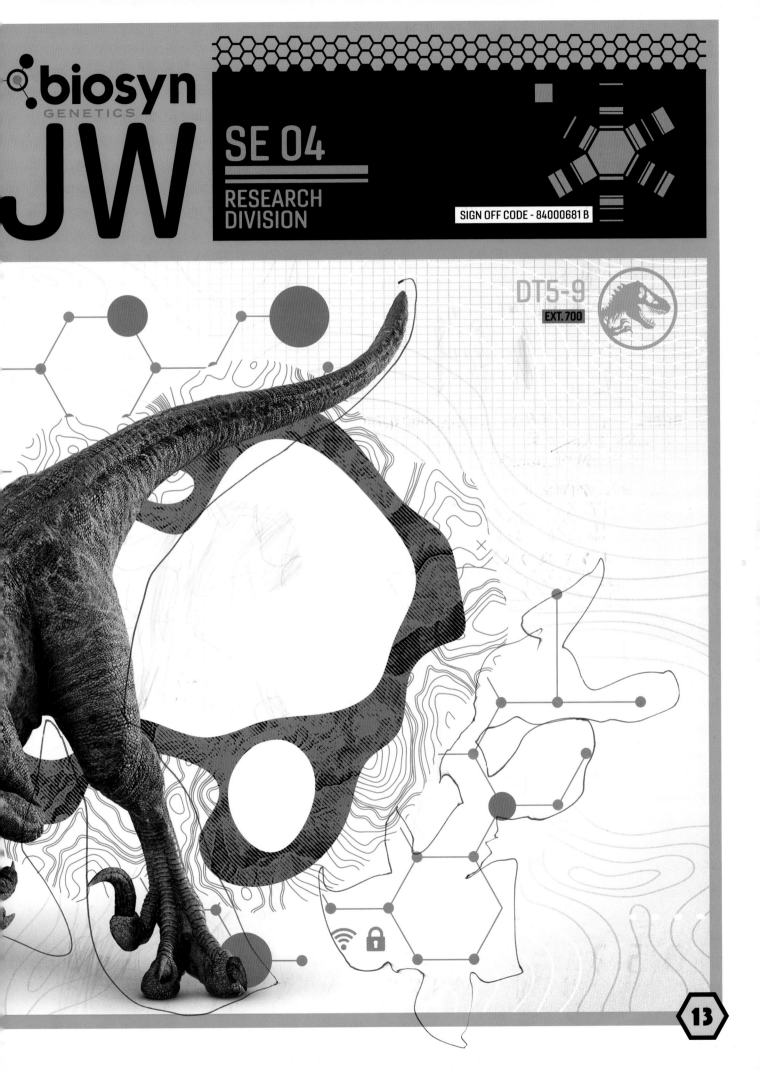

biosyn
GENETICS
JW

SE 04

RESEARCH
DIVISION

SIGN OFF CODE - 84000681 B

DT5-9

EXT. 700

13

BETA AND BLUE MAZE

Solve the maze to help Blue find her way back to her genetic clone, Beta.

START

FINISH

ANSWERS ON PAGE 60

WELCOME TO THE WILD

How many dinosaurs can you find hiding in this wilderness scene? Circle each dinosaur you find, and write the totals in the boxes below.

ANSWERS ON PAGE 60

MEET... T. REX

The legendary apex predator never backs down from a fight. Her bite is unmatched – she can drive her thick, serrated teeth into the toughest of hides and shatter bones. Can she defend her title as the largest land carnivore of all time?

DINOSAUR INDEX

T.REX

BREED: *TYRANNOSAURUS REX* (TIE-RAN-OH-SAWR-US REX)
MEANING: KING TYRANT LIZARD
FAMILY: TYRANNOSAURIDAE

AGGRESSION: HIGH

INTELLIGENCE: MODERATE

LENGTH
13.5 M (44.29 ft)

HEIGHT
5.2 M (17.06 ft)

HEIGHT
1.88 M (6.16 ft)

WEIGHT
8.4 tonnes (18,518 lbs)

FOOTPRINT

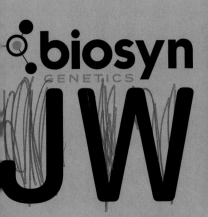
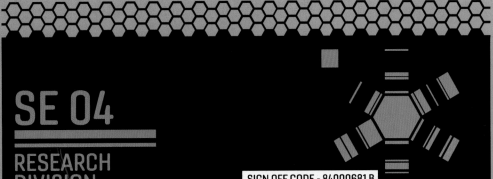

biosyn
GENETICS

JW

SE 04

RESEARCH
DIVISION

SIGN OFF CODE - 84000681 B

ran

OSUM
CODE

DTS-9-6

EXT. 700

Maq

17

T. REX

FIND THE DINOSAUR NAMES

Find and circle the names of dinosaurs that can be found near the Biosyn Genetics compound.

ALLOSAURUS ☐   BARYONYX ☐   CARNOTAURUS ☐

DILOPHOSAURUS ☐   GIGANOTOSAURUS ☐   PARASAUROLOPHUS ☐   QUETZALCOATLUS ☐

D	A	G	A	X	R	C	A	H	F	A	X	R	C	W	P	T	A	Y	D
S	G	I	G	A	N	O	T	O	S	A	U	R	U	S	A	G	Q	H	I
X	C	A	V	Z	E	F	A	G	S	V	C	X	E	W	R	V	U	C	L
Z	W	X	G	V	B	Y	T	R	Q	D	G	G	H	J	A	B	E	J	O
A	L	L	O	S	A	U	R	U	S	A	X	B	C	H	S	U	T	I	P
Q	E	R	C	D	S	C	B	N	L	K	J	G	A	E	A	B	Z	A	H
V	M	L	I	U	X	C	V	B	A	V	X	T	F	A	U	C	A	V	O
Z	Q	W	E	D	C	B	Z	X	E	V	R	A	T	Y	R	X	L	A	S
A	R	A	D	S	X	A	E	A	C	Y	S	R	T	X	O	R	C	P	A
C	V	W	Y	R	C	R	B	U	E	Y	Z	V	E	C	L	E	O	O	U
R	F	C	V	X	V	Y	G	H	X	B	O	X	X	F	O	F	A	I	R
E	A	I	R	A	A	O	R	F	C	Z	Z	Y	U	I	P	F	T	U	U
L	J	R	C	P	L	N	U	I	R	D	T	R	T	H	H	S	L	G	S
A	K	C	B	D	C	Y	Y	G	F	X	X	E	R	Y	U	X	U	B	Y
F	R	A	X	E	C	X	F	W	D	S	E	S	C	S	S	V	S	V	C
X	S	C	F	X	Z	A	F	C	A	R	N	O	T	A	U	R	U	S	K

ANSWERS ON PAGE 60

19

MEET... GIGANOTOSAURUS

The largest known terrestrial carnivore, this massive apex predator is larger than *T. rex*. The massive *Giganotosaurus* can reach speeds of up to 48 kph (30 mph) and is the most formidable threat to everyone and everything in the Biosyn Valley. He is unstoppable and destroys everything in his path. What do you think would happen if he comes face to face with another apex predator like *T. rex*?

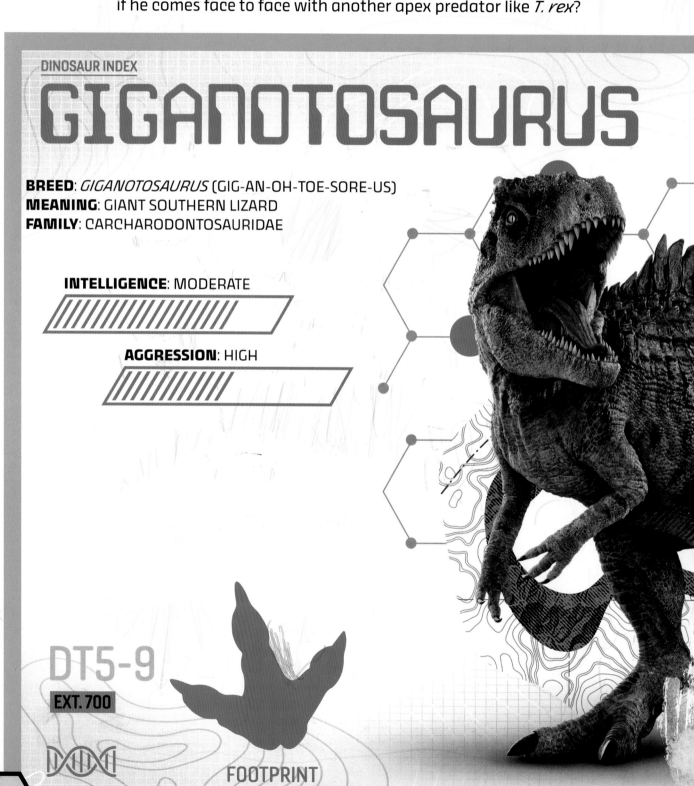

DINOSAUR INDEX

GIGANOTOSAURUS

BREED: *GIGANOTOSAURUS* (GIG-AN-OH-TOE-SORE-US)
MEANING: GIANT SOUTHERN LIZARD
FAMILY: CARCHARODONTOSAURIDAE

INTELLIGENCE: MODERATE

AGGRESSION: HIGH

DT5-9

EXT. 700

FOOTPRINT

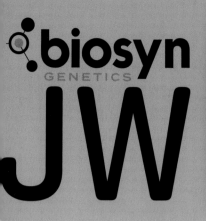

biosyn
GENETICS

JW

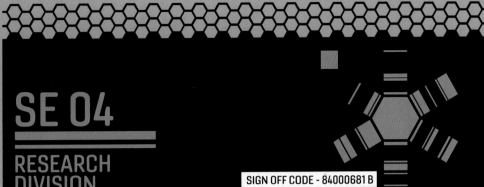

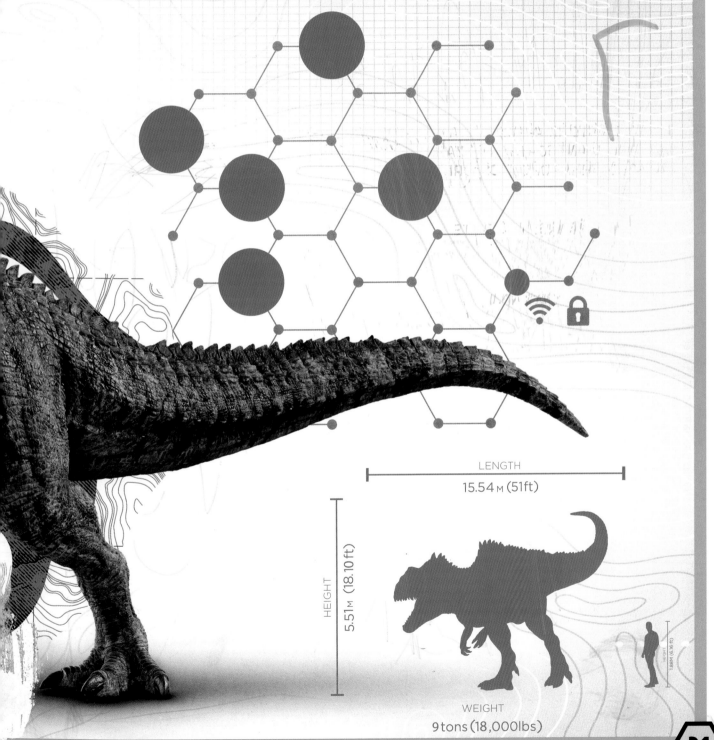

LENGTH
15.54 M (51ft)

HEIGHT
5.51M (18.10ft)

WEIGHT
9tons (18,000lbs)

HEIGHT 1.88M (6.16 ft)

DOT-TO-DOT

Starting at number 1, connect the dots to complete the picture of *Giganotosaurus*, then colour it in.

CRACK THE CODE

Use the legend below to decode the password and shut down the Biosyn Genetics security system.

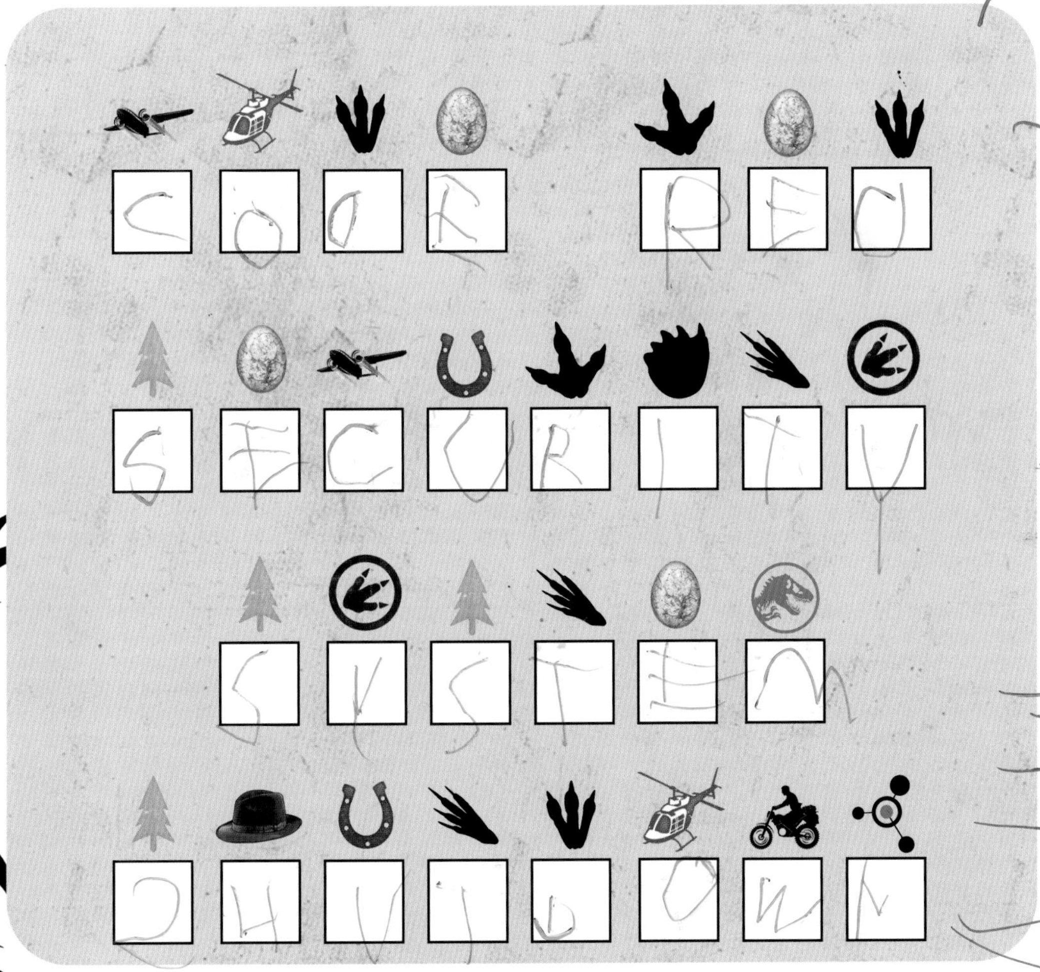

ANSWERS ON PAGE 60

CODE LEGEND

C
H
N
S
W
D
I
O
T
Y
E
M
R
U

DINOSAUR SCRAMBLE

Unscramble the words below

MEABR SMEIN

_ _ _ _ _   _ _ _ _ _

OD ONT UIRDTBS

_ _   _ _ _   _ _ _ _ _ _ _

ERDGNA

_ _ _ _ _ _

SEENICC

_ _ _ _ _ _ _

ANSWERS ON PAGE 60

SCIENTIFIC SEQUENCE

Using the paths, trasnfer the letters into the boxes below to unscramble the word.

C A E E R R H S

R E C E A R C H

TRACK THE DINOSAUR

Follow the directions to track down the dinosaur.

START HERE

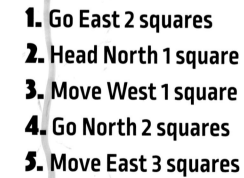

1. Go East 2 squares
2. Head North 1 square
3. Move West 1 square
4. Go North 2 squares
5. Move East 3 squares
6. Head South 3 squares

26

ANSWERS ON PAGE 60

MEET... QUETZALCOATLUS

Named after the Aztec feathered serpent god, the *Quetzalcoatlus* is a pterosaur and is one of the biggest known flying animals of all time. She has a long, stiff neck and a massive wingspan of 11 m (36 ft) – wide enough to park two cars on, but that's not recommended! This gigantic creature commands the skies over Biosyn Valley. Although toothless, the *Quetzalcoatlus* uses its sharp beak as a deadly weapon and will swallow anything it can fit down its giant throat.

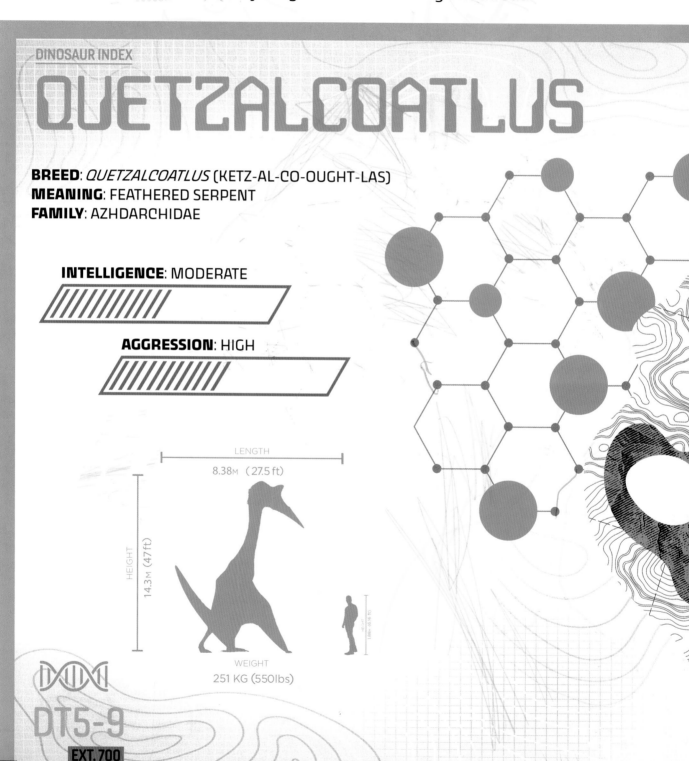

DINOSAUR INDEX

QUETZALCOATLUS

BREED: *QUETZALCOATLUS* (KETZ-AL-CO-OUGHT-LAS)
MEANING: FEATHERED SERPENT
FAMILY: AZHDARCHIDAE

INTELLIGENCE: MODERATE

AGGRESSION: HIGH

LENGTH
8.38M (27.5 ft)

HEIGHT
14.3M (47 ft)

HEIGHT 1.88m (6.16 ft)

WEIGHT
251 KG (550lbs)

DT5-9

EXT. 700

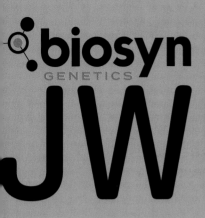

biosyn
GENETICS

JW

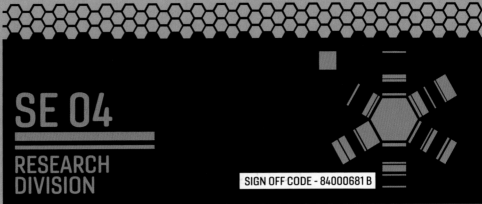

SE 04
RESEARCH
DIVISION

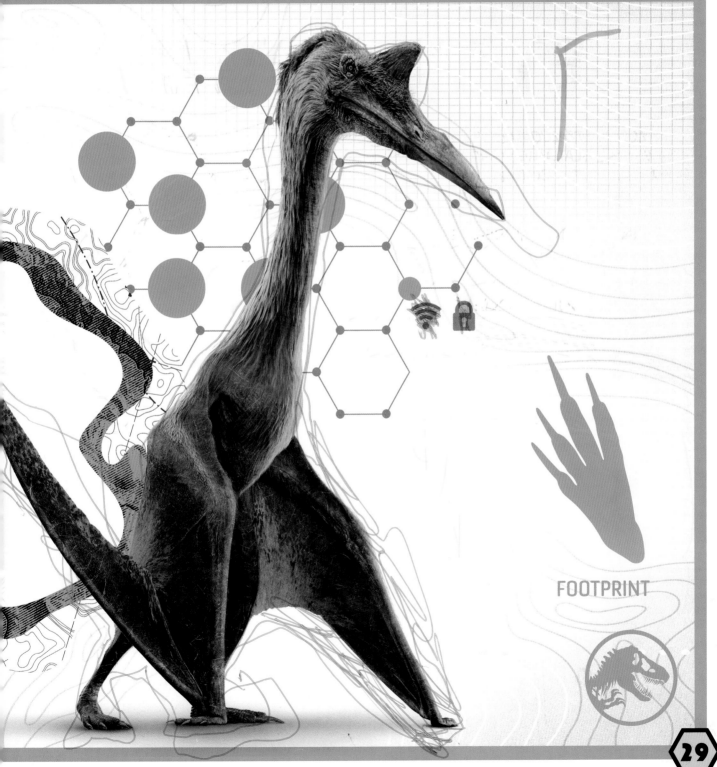

FOOTPRINT

SPOT THE DIFFERENCE

See if you can spot all six differences between these two pictures.

ANSWERS ON PAGE 60

AT THE BIOSYN GENETICS LAB

Find and circle the names of items that can be found in the Biosyn Genetics laboratory in the word search below. The words can be horizontal, vertical, backwards or diagonal.

DNA ☒   CLONING ☐   AMBER ☐

MICROSCOPE ☐   GOGGLES ☐   COMPUTER ☐   MONITOR ☐

G	F	A	R	O	T	I	N	O	M	X	J
H	D	V	U	J	B	G	L	Q	D	G	H
J	D	B	N	H	N	O	K	C	F	E	C
R	D	N	C	B	V	G	J	L	C	P	M
V	X	R	A	X	J	G	V	O	G	O	A
C	M	L	I	X	C	L	N	N	F	C	F
A	Q	E	D	C	B	E	U	I	R	S	B
Z	R	A	A	X	A	S	P	N	D	O	T
R	A	M	B	E	R	B	L	G	S	R	N
I	F	G	X	S	D	G	H	X	A	C	X
Q	S	R	H	Q	O	R	T	Z	X	I	C
L	C	O	M	P	U	T	E	R	E	M	W

HIDDEN MESSAGE

Cross out the word BEWARE every time you see it in the box. When you reach a letter that does not belong, write it below to reveal the message.

```
B E W A R E T T B E W
A R E R B E W A R E E
E B E W A R E X B E
W A R E Z B E W A R
E O B E W A R E N B
E W A R E E B E W A
```

ANSWERS ON 61

WARNING

BEWARE
OF THE
T.REX

NOT RESPONSIBLE FOR
INJURY OR DEATHS

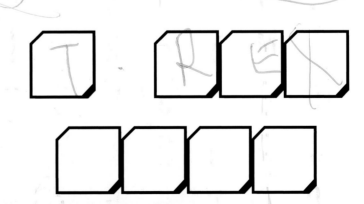

MEET... THERIZINOSAURUS

This grey and black feathered dinosaur weighs 5 tonnes and has a 7 m (24 ft) long neck. It's gigantic, razor-sharp claws are the size of baseball bats, making them the longest of any known animal. Luckily, you'll probably hear it before you see it as its distinctive sound echoes throughout Biosyn Valley. Despite being an herbivore, the *Therizinosaurus's* ability to slash through anything makes her a true threat to any predator.

DINOSAUR INDEX

THERIZINOSAURUS

BREED: *THERIZINOSAURUS* (THER-IH-ZEEN-OH-SOR-US)
MEANING: SCYTHE LIZARD
FAMILY: THERIZINOSAURIDAE

INTELLIGENCE: LOW

AGGRESSION: LOW

FOOTPRINT

LENGTH
9.4m (31ft)

HEIGHT
6.85m (22.5ft)

WEIGHT
5 TONS (10,000 lbs)

DT5-9

EXT. 700

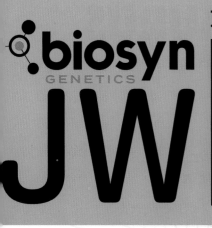

biosyn
GENETICS

JW

SE 04

RESEARCH DIVISION

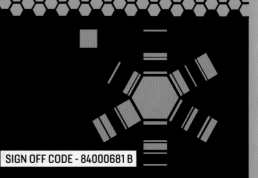

SIGN OFF CODE - 84000681 B

CLASSIFIED

35

DRAW THERIZINOSAURUS

Copy *Therizinosaurus* on the next page using the grid below as a guide. You may find it easiest to draw one square at a time.

MEET... DIMETRODON

The *Dimetrodon* is a low-to-the-ground, crocodile-like reptile with a huge frilled back fin that's three times its own height. Its ear-piercing screeches and shrieks are especially frightening close up as it stalks our heroes deep in the underground Amber Mines of Biosyn Valley. Its conical teeth are perfect for gripping slippery fish and amphibians.

DINOSAUR INDEX

DIMETRODON

BREED: *DIMETRODON* (DIE-MET-RO-DON)
MEANING: TWO MEASURES OF TEETH
FAMILY: SPHENACODONTIDAE

INTELLIGENCE: LOW

AGGRESSION: MODERATE

FOOTPRINT

DT5-9 EXT. 700

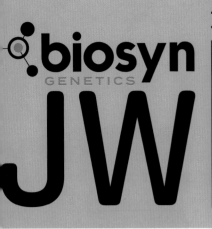

LENGTH
4.11M (13.4ft)

HEIGHT
1.76M (5.8ft)

HEIGHT
1.88M (6.16 ft)

WEIGHT
226 KG (500 lbs)

LOST IN THE AMBER MINE

Solve the maze by leading the cart through the Amber Mine.
Avoid the hissing *Dimetrodons*!

START

FINISH

ANSWERS ON PAGE 61

BIOTECHNOLOGY SUDOKU

Fill in the grid so that every row, every column and every 4x4 box contains one of each symbol.

ANSWERS ON PAGE 61

MEET... PYRORAPTOR

This small, bird-like dinosaur has large, curved claws on the second toe of each foot. Fully covered in bright red feathers, the *Pyroraptor* stalks his prey throughout the varied terrain and climates of Biosyn Valley. From the dense jungle to the snow-covered mountains, his stealth movements enable this deadly predator to sneak up on prey. He can even hunt its targets from underneath the icy waters of a frozen lake, waiting for his victims to fall through the cracking ice above.

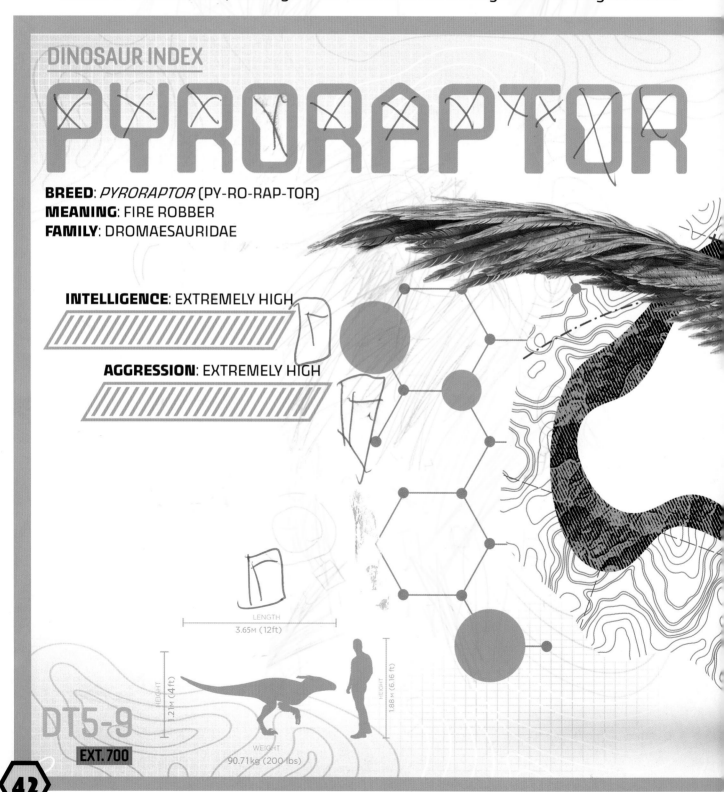

DINOSAUR INDEX

PYRORAPTOR

BREED: *PYRORAPTOR* (PY-RO-RAP-TOR)
MEANING: FIRE ROBBER
FAMILY: DROMAESAURIDAE

INTELLIGENCE: EXTREMELY HIGH

AGGRESSION: EXTREMELY HIGH

LENGTH
3.65M (12ft)

HEIGHT
1.2M (4ft)

HEIGHT
1.88M (6.16 ft)

WEIGHT
90.71kg (200 lbs)

DT5-9

EXT. 700

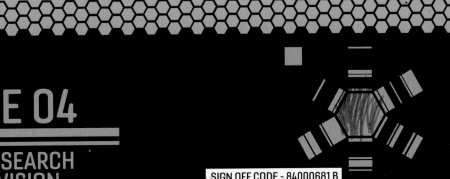

biosyn
GENETICS

JW

SE 04

RESEARCH DIVISION

SIGN OFF CODE - 84000681 B

FOOTPRINT

CLASSIFIED

COLOUR BY NUMBER

Use the colour key below to bring this *Pyroraptor* to life!

COLOUR KEY ► **1** **2** **3** **4** **5**

DINING ON THE FOREST FLOOR

Match the dinosaurs to their footprints. Draw a line and follow the footprints to lead them to the same dinosaur species.

ANSWERS ON PAGE 61

45

INTERLOCKED
Use the words below to complete the puzzle.

DANGER ☑   GENETICS ☑   PRESERVE ☑

PROTECT ☑   T. REX ☑   ZONE ☑

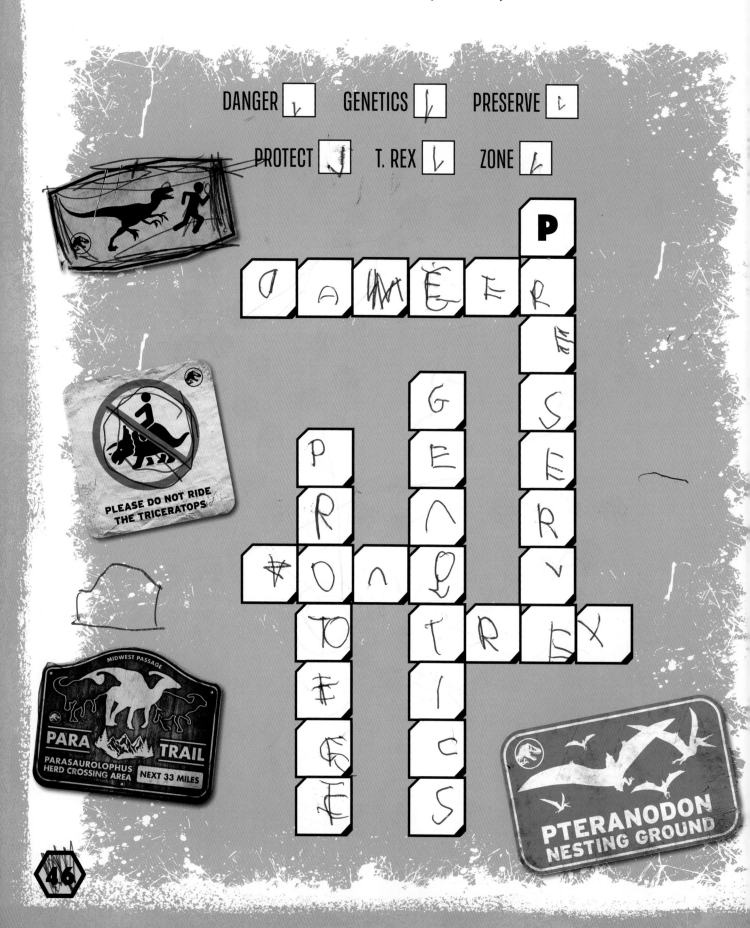

PLEASE DO NOT RIDE
THE TRICERATOPS

MIDWEST PASSAGE

PARA ▲ TRAIL
PARASAUROLOPHUS
HERD CROSSING AREA   NEXT 33 MILES

PTERANODON
NESTING GROUND

Make sure you ask a grown-up before using scissors.

49

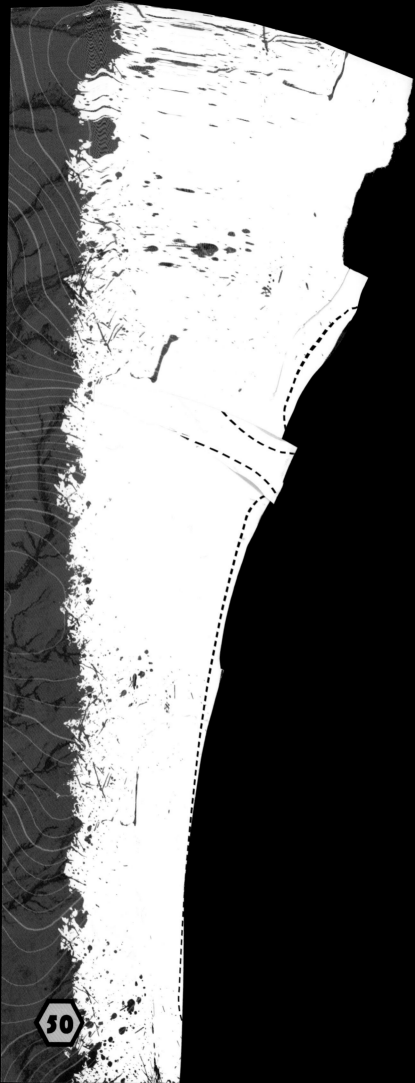

SHADOW MATCH

Find the dinosaur that matches the shadow and then colour in the drawings.

ANSWERS ON PAGE 61

A

B

C

D

MEET... DILOPHOSAURUS

Small but extremely venomous, the *Dilophosaurus* has a brilliant-coloured crest that flanks its head. The *Dilophosaurus* moves with agile, snake-like movements and can appear as if it's smiling as it stalks its prey. But in an instant, this deadly predator can pop up and snap open its neck frill, as it hisses and spits a deadly black venom at its victims. It uses its arms and claws to grip prey before it bites down with its razor-sharp teeth.

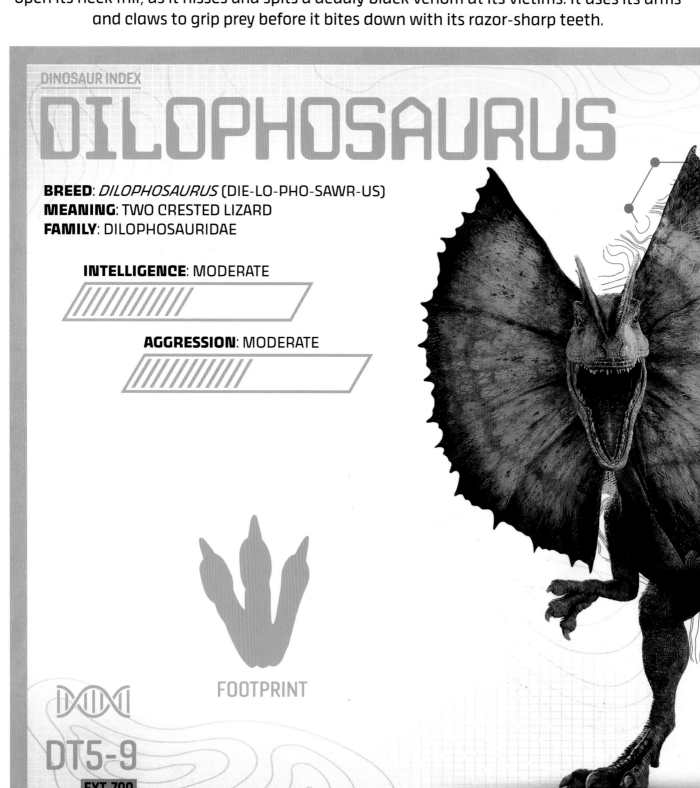

DINOSAUR INDEX

DILOPHOSAURUS

BREED: *DILOPHOSAURUS* (DIE-LO-PHO-SAWR-US)
MEANING: TWO CRESTED LIZARD
FAMILY: DILOPHOSAURIDAE

INTELLIGENCE: MODERATE

AGGRESSION: MODERATE

FOOTPRINT

DT5-9

EXT. 700

biosyn
GENETICS

JW

SE 04

RESEARCH DIVISION

SIGN OFF CODE - 84000681 B

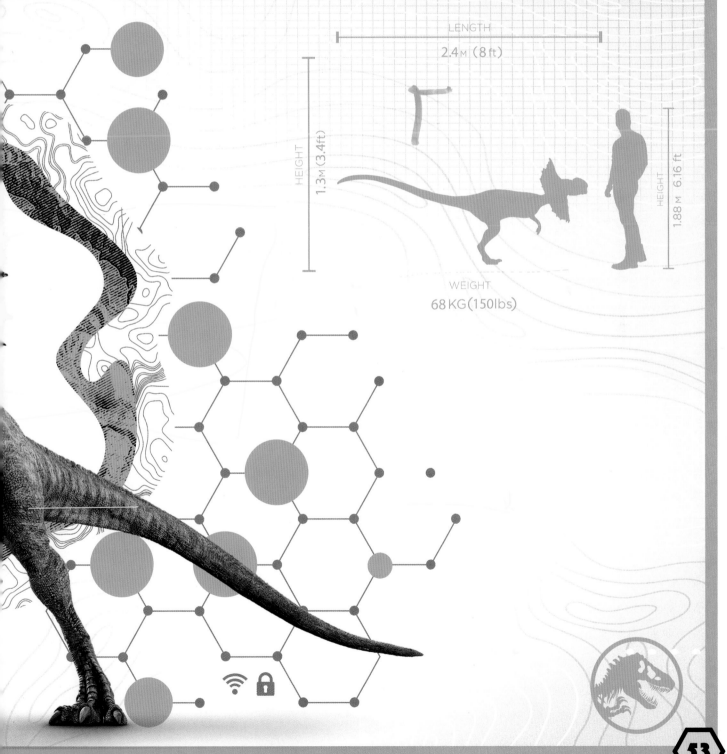

LENGTH
2.4 M (8 ft)

HEIGHT
1.3 M (3.4ft)

HEIGHT
1.88 M 6.16 ft

WEIGHT
68 KG (150lbs)

RETURN TO NATURE

A new day dawns in the valley. Find and circle the dinosaurs hidden in the picture.

FIND:

MEET... PARASAUROLOPHUS

This gentle herbivore socialises in a herd, which makes it easier to detect the presence of danger. It uses its head crest to make foghorn-type sounds to warn the herd of a nearby predator. Owen Grady rounds up a herd of *Parasaurolophuses* on horseback, using a lasso to rope any runaways. He drives the herd to a fresh feeding ground, where they eat plants and chew on rotting wood.

DINOSAUR INDEX

PARASAUROLOPHUS

BREED: *PARASAUROLOPHUS* (PAR-AH-SAWR-OLL-OH-FUSS)
MEANING: NEAR CRESTED LIZARD
FAMILY: LAMBEOSAURIDAE

INTELLIGENCE: LOW

AGGRESSION: LOW

FOOTPRINT

DT5-9

EXT. 700

LENGTH
7.5M (24.6ft)

HEIGHT
3M (9.8ft)

WEIGHT
2.6 tons (5,700 lbs)

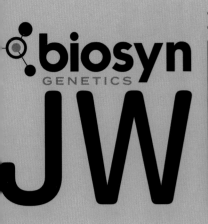

JW

SE 04

RESEARCH DIVISION

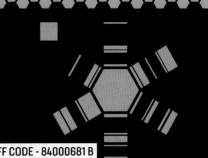

SIGN OFF CODE - 84000681 B

HERDING DINOSAURS

Owen and the Department of Fish and Wildlife need your help! They need to drive a herd of *Parasaurolophuses* across the range. Grab a dice, a friend or two and a counter for each player and see who can get the herd to the fresh feeding ground first.

START

1 | **2** | **3** The herd is moving fast. Move forward three spaces. | **7** A juvenile *Parasaurolophus* has run off. Go back to the start.

4 | **5** | **6**

27 | **26** | **25** Stop for a snack. Miss a turn. | **24** | **23**

28

29 You're galloping ahead. Take another turn.

30 | **31**

HOW TO PLAY:

1. The youngest player goes first.
2. Take it in turns to throw the dice and move around the board.
3. If you land on a space with text, follow the instructions.
4. If you land on a dinosaur footprint space, take an extra turn.
5. The first player to reach the FINISH is the winner.

8

9

10

11

12

13
The herd is startled by a noise from the woods. Miss a turn.

14

15

21

20

19
The herd has stopped to graze. Move back four spaces.

22
The herd crosses a stream. Move forwards one space.

18

17

16
You lasso a runaway dinosaur. Move forward two spaces.

32

33
The dinosaurs are distracted. Throw a six to move on.

34

35

FINISH

ANSWERS

WORD SEARCH
PAGE 10

```
D B I O N M A Q Z D X H
E K C I Z W L R X A T A
S K A M U A A S L M Z S
C G K Y S R N B X A C T
V B G L O R Q T I O S
O W E N S A M G S S T O
X Z V R C P E M M I K R
H J A D U R A K R E T Z
Y Z E Q S S B U A E U
T S D A E E I A N P L C
J R L T Z B G H J K A Q
Z C S C V B E L L I E S
```

BETA AND BLUE MAZE
PAGE 14

START

FINISH

WELCOME TO THE WILD
PAGE 15

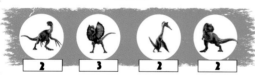

| 2 | 3 | 2 | 2 |

FIND THE DINOSAUR NAMES
PAGE 19

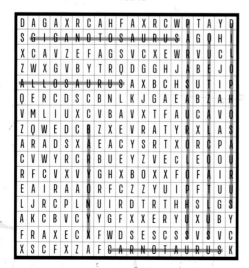

```
D A G A X R C A H F A X R C W P T A Y D
S G I G A N O T O S A U R U S A G Q H I
X C A V Z E F A G S V C X E W R V U C L
Z W X G V B Y T R Q D G G H J A B E J O
A L L O S A U R U S A X B C H S U T I P
Q E R C D S C B N L K J G A E A B Z A H
V M L I U X C V B A V X T F A U C A W N
Z Q W E D C B Z X E V A T Y R X L A S
A R A D S X A E A C Y S R T X O R C P A
C V W Y R C R B U E Y Z V E C L E Q Q U
R F C V T S V H G H X B O X X F O F A I
R E A I R A A O R F C Z Z Y U I P F T U
L J R C P L N U I R D T R T H H S L G S
A K C B V C Y Y G F X X E R Y U X U B Y
F R A X E C A F W D S E S C S S V S V C
X S C F X Z A F C A R N O T A U R U S K
```

CRACK THE CODE
PAGE 23

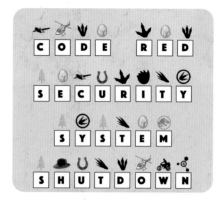

C O D E **R E D**

S E C U R I T Y

S Y S T E M

S H U T D O W N

DINO SCRAMBLE
PAGE 24

AMBER MINES

DO NOT DISTURB

DANGER

SCIENCE

SCIENTIFIC SEQUENCE
PAGE 25

R E S E A R C H

TRACK THE DINOSAUR
PAGE 26

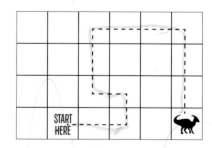

START HERE

SPOT THE DIFFERENCE
PAGE 30-31

ANSWERS

AT THE BOISYN GENETICS LAB
PAGE 32

G	F	A	R	O	T	I	N	O	M	X	J
H	D	V	U	J	B	G	L	Q	D	G	H
J	D	B	N	H	N	O	K	C	F	E	C
R	D	N	C	B	V	G	J	L	C	P	M
V	X	R	A	X	J	G	V	O	G	O	A
C	M	L	I	X	C	L	N	N	F	C	F
A	Q	E	D	C	B	E	U	I	R	S	B
Z	R	A	A	X	S	P	N	D	O	T	
R	A	M	B	E	R	B	L	G	S	R	N
I	F	G	X	S	D	G	H	X	A	C	X
Q	S	R	H	Q	O	R	T	Z	X	I	C
L	C	O	M	P	U	T	E	R	E	M	W

HIDDEN MESSAGE
PAGE 33

T REX
ZONE

LOST IN THE AMBER MINE
PAGE 40

BIOTECHNOLOGY SUDOKU
PAGE 41

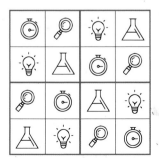

DINING ON THE FOREST FLOOR
PAGE 45

INTERLOCKED
PAGE 46

SHADOW MATCH
PAGE 51

C

RETURN TO NATURE
PAGE 54-55